"Words are the daughter of earth"

G. Johnson

A Walk to the
Center of Things:
poems by
Nils Peterson

cæsura editions

To Jim who keeps things together — fondly Nils

(poetry center san josé)

Also by Nils Peterson:

Here Is No Ordinary Rejoicing

The Comedy of Desire

Water, Fire, Earth, and Air
A limited fine print edition, with artwork by Patrick Surgalski

Driving a Herd of Moose to Durango

For This Day

The Revenge of the Socks

A Walk to the Center of Things:

poems by

Nils Peterson

cæsura editions

A Walk to the Center of Things
© 2011 Nils Peterson
all art © Patrick Surgalski
All rights reserved
Printed in the United States of America

A Cæsura Edition
First Printing

A project of Poetry Center San José

Executive Editor and Project Manager, Erica Goss
Art by Patrick Surgalski
Design by Joe Miller

Peterson, Nils, 1933 –
A Walk to the Center of Things

ISBN: 978-1-61170-027-5
Library of Congress Cataloging-in-Publication Data
Library of Congress Control Number: 2011927915

Cæsura Editions is a trademark of Poetry Center San José
www.pcsj.org

Printed on recycled 55# acid free paper and meets all ANSI standards
for archival quality paper.
Set in Baskerville Monotype with heads in Mrs. Eaves.

Published by:

Robertson Publishing
59 N. Santa Cruz Avenue, Suite B.
Los Gatos, California 95030 USA
www.RobertsonPublishing.com

Dedication

Fifty years ago I was standing mallet in hand by a croquet court at the Breadloaf Writers Conference needing a partner. A young woman, also a waiter, walked by. She was wearing Bermuda shorts. Two years later, we were married.

This book is dedicated to the great, overarching fact of that marriage, wide enough and long enough to give room to the many small marriages and separations that allowed us to grow.

Contents

More How Things Happen

PREFACE

Poetry Center San José is pleased to offer to its members and to the public at large this collection of poems by one of its founding members, Nils Peterson. Nils Peterson, the first Poet Laureate of Santa Clara County, was chosen because of the many years he spent making poets and poetry available to the public, his encouragement of so many young writers with their writing, and for his own work. This collection of poems confirms the wisdom of that choice.

His volume inaugurates a new series of poetry collections sponsored by PCSJ. It is our way to support poetry in a time when institutional funding is disappearing.

> Kevin Arnold
> President of the Board of Directors
> Poetry Center San José

An Introduction with Thanks

There is a scene in the Odyssey where the hero digs a trench, surrounds it with milk, honey, wine, water, barley, then cuts the throats of a ram and black ewe. Their dark blood falls into the earth wound. Then out of Erebus eager souls erupt, longing to eat and drink, longing to wear again the sweet cloak of flesh.

As I've put this collection together, I've felt a little like Odysseus as the ghosts of my poems gathered around me, each wanting the blood of ink, the flesh of paper, the inclusion of memory. But they could not all fit. You'll remember that he had to crouch before the pit of sacrifice with drawn sword and hold off the many who wanted to speak, for awhile even the shade of his mother. Discrimination is not easy.

It is 2011, my 77th year. The earliest poem in this collection was published in the Beloit Poetry Journal in 1961. So, more than half century of writing poetry.

I wish to offer to all of my poetic attempts thanks. You taught me much. Where we've succeeded, you've left me pleased. Where I've failed, you've shown me what I must learn.

And my particular gratitude goes to those poems that are here included. Sometimes you have made me see myself embarrassingly clearly. Sometimes you've preserved for me in the amber of syllables, a person or a moment. Sometimes you have shown me the shining of the world. Sometimes you have shown me where the world isn't shining. That too one needs to know.

And so my friends, my poems, my thanks.

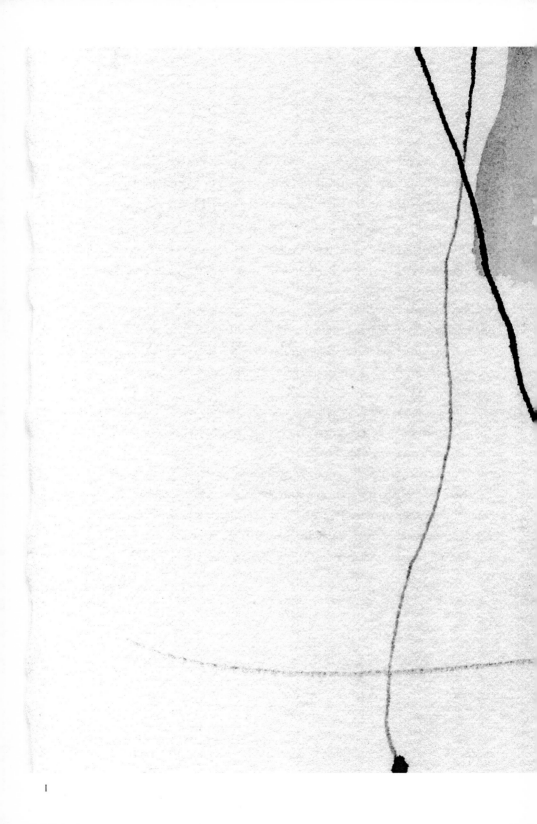

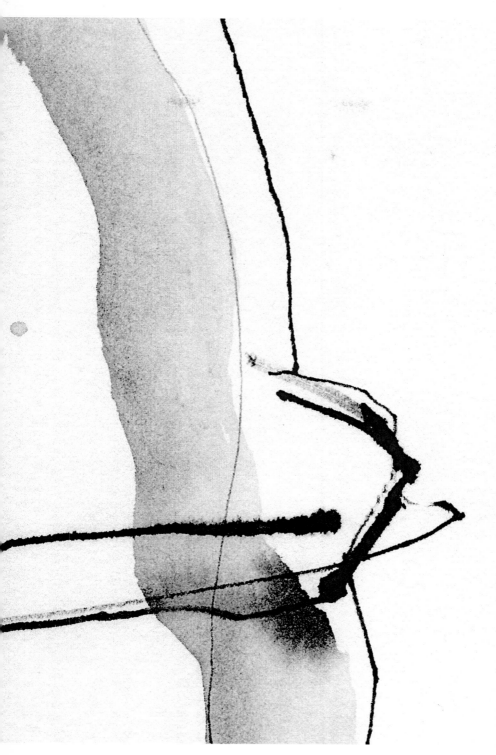

THE BUS

Sunny day. June. California. But I'm in New Jersey. November night. Standing in the cold with my mother waiting for a bus on the corner of Front Street and Watchung Avenue, the bright window of a cafe shining square behind us where hot dogs, bright as pumpkins, go round and round on a rolling grill. At its side, exotic, unSwedish jars of yellow mustard and green relish glisten. I stand jigging from one foot to another, cold and salivating. The night is black, and though there are store lights and street lights, unilluminated. It is 1939.

Around the corner lives the ice cream parlor where sometimes after mother had bought something at the Surprise Store which pleased her, she'd buy me a cone and I'd order rum raisin with a delicious sense of sin. Down the street is the newspaper store run by the two weird brothers, (one limped left and one limped right) where I had my first sip of Coca Cola. It was from my father's glass. No styrofoam. A Coca Cola glass, pleasingly shaped and emblazoned with curling script in white. No drink better, ever.

A couple of blocks away lurks the Plainfield Courier News where in 15 years I'll work in the circulation department for 35 bucks a week, but now I'm cold and hungry, no hot dog, and the bus, the bus, the bus—is not coming, will never come, will never take me where I want to go. No. Never!

The Reading Room

had at its center an enormous globe that showed the way the
world was. It turned as easily about its expensive spindle as the world itself
and I spun it slowly, exploring place after place, each country with a color
defining its "I amness." How much blue the sea took to get its proper share.

Sometimes I would sit in the room and read my books for awhile
before roller skating home on the streets that had the smoothest sidewalks
so the wheels clamped to my shoes with a key would not catch on a tree-
root-propped slab, tear loose, and send me tumbling to another scraped
knee. Sometimes I'd finish my book and return it before setting off from the
friendly silence.

The room was high-ceilinged, tall-windowed, square, with a
square of leather-cushioned chairs surrounding the globe. *This is how I want
to live,* I felt rather than said, *in a solid, permanent, somewhat dustily elegant place,
with the round certainty of the way things are before me.*

This was sixty years ago and more. Only the blue of the sea has
stayed itself. Now the whole old globe with its intricate, pattern of forgotten
countries rests, a curiosity, in the back room of the antique shop of the
world. Maybe the library still stands, though most of the books I read have
long ago disintegrated or disappeared.

The boy who sat there reading whispers to me sometimes. He tries
to tell me what was. I listen, nod, but cannot tell him what will be.

WALKING TO SCHOOL

Autumn, and, I, not an especially triumphant
boy, walked in triumph down a street lined
with torches, fiery yellows, shiny oranges, fierce
reds lit up for me. From Hillside Avenue,
I descended down Evergreen lined with maples
from sidewalk to the curb. When the rains came,
heavy leaves fell, and I strode on gold, soggy,
but like the streets of heaven. Home owners who
didn't sweep quickly possessed a sidewalk abstract
etched by leaf.

      Brown November. Homeward
in early dark, breathing the acid smell
of burning leaves, admiring the men leaning
on iron-tined rakes, tending the smoky pyres.

A Thing of Beauty

My father could not give it away, the Stromberg Carlson, when the tubes failed – the age of the console radio had passed – nor could he throw it away because the wood was so beautiful. He who had worked in a cabinet maker's shop as a young man, loved the grain of hardwoods with his eye and hand. So it was moved into my bedroom where it sat, a mahogany god no one heard.

When I grew older, I hid books, risque, not pornographic – Thorne Smith, *The Affairs of Bel Ami*, Guy De Maupassant and the like – in among the tubes, my secret cave-like the mine where the Lone Ranger cast his silver bullets.

For my thirteenth birthday, my parents thought a reader like me could use a desk. So, in the night, they came and carried out the radio to put in the desk. My books fell on the floor like original sin. The beginning of my fourteenth year was not a happy one – my delights confiscated. As I walked about the house, I felt as if I had been exiled to an obscure, but Lutheran, Elba. I knew then, I'd never fit into a desk job.

Later I found the books in my father's own secret cave, up in the the ceiling boards of the basement. So, I had another, though not public, lending library.

Maybe the books were like the radio – something in them so beautiful, my father could not throw them away.

SANDLOTS

Thinking of my boyhood one – not long before
a Victory Garden – the ground uneven with the ghosts
of furrows past. The outfield tilted up to the street.
No level playing field here. There were those
who could play and those who played anyway.

Over the fence was a home run at first, then,
a double – when most of us could clear the fence,
an out. In truth, it was a pain, the left fielder
scrambling over the railing to chase the ball
before it started rolling down the hill.
If you didn't get it quick, it could go a quarter
of a mile. We learned to swing level, to try
to meet the center of the ball for a line drive,
or a little above for a sharp grounder made mean
by the hard-packed, lumpy earth. It was nothing
but Zen. At last the playing field felt as tight
as last year's sports jacket, and we set out
into the great world to find a larger.

But now I'm thinking of poetry, of life, of my life,
of the fact there are no sandlots anymore and what
it means to try for singles instead of swinging
for the fences. I'm thinking of the Vossler brothers,
of Joe Mosca and his father who would take me
to Yankee Stadium on the subway, I'm thinking
of Joe Dimaggio, his lovely long stride along the plate
into the ball and the whip crack of his arms as they
swung around, thinking of my brother Bill, and George
Hamilton who lived across the street but never played

anything except bagpipe music on an old Victrola.
I'm thinking now of Tommy Heinrich, "Old Reliable,"
whom the Yankees could count on for a single
when there were runners on base. I'm thinking
of this poem, wondering if it might skip through the hole
between first and second to send someone home.

First Kiss. Remembering Bessie Diehl

I was dared into it – maybe by Gibson Brown whose
girl she was if she was anyone's girl. New Year's Eve,
maybe, but not midnight. I gave a little peck. I was nothing
if not polite. She said, "So that's it?" So I tried again.

I feel again the softness of her lips and the arching
yield of her back and the way I felt touched along
my whole length. I plummeted down into my body
from wherever I usually lived. She closed her eyes

going somewhere I couldn't imagine. I kept mine
open, watching. Something in her was so certain,
so sure, so different – none of the boastful,
hard, boy-talk had prepared me for that.

On the Nature of Exposition

Exposition

He's sitting in the Corner Tavern adding a couple of lonely beers to his tab. In comes Herb: "Nils, Let's go to the races." "Got no money." "Come anyway." "Got six bucks for the next two weeks." "Come anyway." "Where are you going?" "Yonkers." "Don't know anything about trotters." "Come anyway."

So, up the pike, through the tunnel, along the Hudson. For Nils it's two bucks to get in. Two bucks lost on the first race. His last two brings back ten, so he bets five and a twenty comes home and he's flying. Soon bills bulge his pockets. He's betting tens, then twenties and they come spinning back in a fine English bringing friends. On the last race he bets fifty to win at 8 to 1 and comes in second by a nose, but he's still three or four hundred ahead.

On the way back, they hit a couple of bars, those jazz bars in the Fifties that used to be in the Fifties and Nils is buying for any stranger with a smile. They need to eat. Off to the Stage Delicatessen where Herb, a playwright, knows everybody, so, soon Nils is buying champagne and pastrami sandwiches for a swarm of chorus girls.

Next morning, he wakes up in the Village—last night's horses running with their races again inside his skull, his mouth their stable—with less than fifty bucks in his pocket. Later, walking carefully down the sobering street trying not to jog anything, he says to himself: Give me a sign, a token, some real thing to mark this winning.

Passing Barney's Big Men's Town—Bargains—and there on the "plain pipe racks" a seersucker suit in 44 extra-long for $38.75, so he brings it on home, on the bus.

The Action

Summer school. California. 1965. Walking across campus—young teacher in a seersucker suit jacket, unlikely remains of unlikely winnings at the Yonkers Raceway. He wears a dull, striped, polyester tie. He is thinking about the short story, opening paragraphs, the where, who, and what of them. He smokes a cigar, nerves before class.

And now: a gout of wind, and now: his tie billows out and settles on the ash-deep fire riding above his index and middle fingers, and Now!— a quarter-sized hole.

Suddenly, his mind is with the birth of weather and the new wind shaking itself loose and setting out from the Sea of Japan, the Sea of Okhotsk, carrying at first low gray wet clouds, and he follows as it crosses Kamatchka, the Bering Straits, the Aleutians, the Kuskokwim Mountains, and curls down towards Coos Bay, Eureka, then along the coast to get here just in time to flip his tie (Is this how change enters our lives? he marvels— it begins last week and far out at sea).

Now it is 1492 and he's off with the Nina, and the Pinta, and the Santa Maria to the New World, and again with Raleigh and Virginia Dare and Indians and the ceremonious inhaling of dried native flora—then slavery and plantations and the Civil War and depressions and soil erosion and crop quotas and subsidies and the ache of his lungs a couple of years before which made him give up the cigarettes he began as a declaration of independence at 16 and switch to the cigar which he now smokes.

Back now to the Carboniferous, the Jurassic, great foresty swamps, heavy hang of leaf and vine, the lumber and swagger of beasts, heavings of earth, flux of continents, sinking of seas, the procession of stars, transmogrifications of bog and flesh into dark diamonds... And now he joins his ancestors as down from the trees they come making custom and discovering—Ah! Fire, and war, science, shortages, substitutes—and, nodding at his parents as they leave the old country to meet in New York in an English for Foreigners class, he hurtles along by way of miners, capitalism, academia, coal tar derivatives, rayon, nylon, and, at long last, polyester, to swing into his own immediate life on the rope of his burnt tie, thinking—any event holds all history, thinking, the first sentence of every story is "Let there be Nils."

POEM FOR OUR WEDDING

The time has come to build our house.
Shall we have walls of soft bamboo,
For floors, reeds woven intricate,
Our gay partitions made of straw
Steeped in art's most subtle dyds,
And hanging from the ceiling mats
Pale lanterns to deceive the night?
Then, when heart rubs heart and sparks
Quick fly to life in our lives' tinder,
So easily we'd build again
What friend could cry catastrophe?

Or shall we use our soul's whole skill,
Employ the best wrights want can buy
To build a house Imperial?
Then if love's very earth should quake
Till heaving fundament breaks like sea
It's pebbles roiled to dusty spume
Our house will ride this roll of rock
As yare as any clipper ship
That tossed all storm-dark night, but found
Dawn planting roses on the shore
Of unimaginable Cathay.

CEREMONY

Erika, Cecily, and KittyCat Charles
All played together without any quarrels.
Erika, the eldest, made them all tea
And served it to Charles and small Cecily.

A KIND OF AUTOBIOGRAPHY

While light wonders whether to start the day, a flash of memory –
easing my way down the narrow steps of Maureen's garden, hand on
Judith's shoulder for balance, a lizard, long as my index finger, looks one
way, then another, and skitters between my legs into the purple ground
cover. Did I mark it at the time? – the way one turns over a corner of a
page of a paperback one's likely not to read again just in case, or did some
morning shadow flicker to startle that image out.

Light flooded through the stair-landing window, fired the cut glass
candy dish, and broke into colors across the low bookcase. Home alone,
that itself enough rapture, but now this world joy. I remember trying to
remember it, fix it, make it stay – what was I, ten? eleven? – so beautiful. I
knew it could not last.

"Summertime, the living is easy" – I rise, pull on shorts, think
"That's it for the day," quoting Leif Hass, the poet's son, whom I've met in
the poem his father writes about "the first morning of steady heat." Each
time I pull on shorts, I think of Leif, and his father listening, remembering,
writing it down.

Yesterday, wearing shorts, playing golf, I hit a bad shot, cursed,
called out, "I'm more to be pitied than censured." My friend asked – where's
that from? – thinking Lear. When I sang the 1890's bar room song, –
"Peterson, you've got to get that stuff out of your head," but I thought of
Frost saying poets get their knowledge not deliberately, but by letting what
will – "stick like burrs" as they "walk in the fields."

My Dog William and the Fence

Friends,
Last night I awoke first to a crash,
then, later, to a strange wheezing sound
creeping in from every corner of the house.
I went to investigate and found that my dog
in his nightly nosings, testing, as always,
the limits, had knocked over the rotting fence
that kept him in the backyard. It fell
in such a way that he could not get back
try as he might and in terror he fled
into the crawl space under the house
where his hot fearful breath filled
everywhere. He would not come out from shame
and fear though I grasped him by his paws
and collar - three o'clock in the morning,
mind, I in my bathrobe, kneeling
in the dust among the crumbling rubble
of my broken fence before an animal deep
in his old fears - he had been left
in the hills by his previous owners
who just moved on, as someone down the road
from where my wife was camping told her
after she woke to find a strange black dog
huddled beside her sleeping bag. Finally,
I got up, dusted myself off, and started
to walk away. He was with me in an instant,
his breath fast, shallow, intense.
I sat with him in the bathroom until
he calmed down and his panicked drool dried
and the blood in the gashes on his muzzle,
then went back to bed - but today I had

to construct a fence - not a great fence,
not a pretty fence, a keep-the-dog in fence,
a fence to be a fence until a real fence
could be made - and I had nothing
to build it with - in fact, I couldn't
even find a gawddam hammer - in a house
where usually unused hammers are to be found
mating in every corner. So it was a day
at the handyman and hardware store
trying to figure out how to keep in
that which I love so that it doesn't
get away or flee under my house
and fill it with panicky breath.

I found a hammer for $3.49, cheaply made,
and rejected it for a staple gun, cheaply made
but expensive, and a 40 ft roll of fancy
chicken wire, twice as much as I needed,
but they wouldn't sell less and I spent
the rest of the day trying to fix up
something between the neighbor's wooden fence
and my stucco wall, finally jamming
an old picnic table against my house
and stapling the wire around it and to
a fairly solid post. No one can see
this corner, so it doesn't have
to be pretty. It just needs to keep
the dog in. I had other things to do,
letters, poems, essays, my income tax -
still undone although the second extension
was running out - and the day was hot,
and I needed to keep coming in for water
whereupon I would read in a horoscope

I had done a year ago which kept telling
me truths I did not want to hear again.
It made the sweaty aggravating fence work
seem almost friendly. Fence up, sausage
and salad supper, late summer twilight.
In that violet hour, I took William, the dog,
for his walk around the percolation ponds
and I jogged slowly and thoughtfully
for the first time in a year. This
     is a life. How to get it all in?

I had decided not to have anything
to drink yesterday trying to get rid of the pub
around my stomach left over from a semester
in England and also a sense that maybe
I shouldn't drink every day, but I had a beer
anyway after I got the fence up, an ale,
brown and savory, with rich slow bubbles
and a sour chocolatey aftertaste and I sat
there with a still scared dog at my feet
feeling myself fixed somewhere between
the crawl space and the mysterious
     imprinting of the stars.

ANDERS, FIRST CONSIDERATIONS

This is tongue which I can push out
and forehead which I can wrinkle.
This is foot which I can push and here
is another one which works the same
way. These are arms. I can wave one,
the other, both, and arms have hands
with clutchers I can open, close. And
these are eyes and these are ears through
which the world comes to me, the sightings
and the rumbles of the big ones, and I
am everything except the world.

LONGING

Steady rain after days of steady rain.
Streams rush downward and lakes release
their fullness to the sea. In the mountains,
earth shifts, sliding downwards, making

its own channels, and the Spirit too lets go
of its high place and slides down. "Sing me
a belly song," it says, tired of string quartets.
No, it wants to sing, not listen, sing

the blues, "The Empty Bed Blues." It wants
to have feet that dance, a solemn shuffle but with
a surprising hitch in the middle. It wants
to sit on a bench in front of the courthouse

on the town square of Sidney, Ohio swopping
stories with any old guy who'll listen.

POEM FOR MY BIRTHDAY

It was my seventieth year to heaven.
Woke for a pee and a listen to the wide world waking,
obligato of mourning dove
above
the sonorous *om* of freeway traffic,
plop of newspapers on moon-dark drives,
coffee in bed
and the writing of dreams.

Then off for a walk
beside an October stream, brisk stride of wife,
trot of small dog,
and my slow, cane-steadied plod,
lungs taking in the moist autumn air,
eyes drinking a wine of thick yellow oak leaves
luminous in the gray morning light,
a brocade of old gold
against a gray sky –
underfoot, gold leaf like the streets of heaven.

A laneful of bicyclists in a fierce
peddling, a panting of joggers paired and single,
a young mother in green tights running
behind a
perambulator
out of which a wide-eyed child peers down
at leaves and feet and legs,
and now up and up at a tall man poling
his high way along

the still path

above the quiet run of a dark stream.

I'm a seventy year old smiling public man,

I think to myself – startled now

by a dart of swallows,

and I wonder if my mother

would think me worth the pangs

of my setting forth – a long labor, forty hours.

"He came out of the flower pot," she said, waking.

A good place to come

from, I think,

No rose I, maybe chrysanthemum.

Continuing inward to a time huge

as the sky above the Big House, I, a chauffeur's

son in a summer garden fall-less,

each fine day a forever

to ride

with tattooed Big Ted in the jolting pick up

across the new-mown fields,

or walking the harbor spit,

an orchestra

of tiny fiddler crabs

scattering before my feet.

My father was big as the summer then,

in his gray suit and flat, black-billed, chauffeur's cap,

ready to chariot the Olympians

about their

mysterious ways,
or in work clothes striding, hero among the men
whose hands he hired to weed the wide lawn, trim hedges,
spread compost, pick pears,
rake gravel,
depression years – any work holy
when every day was a holiday – unwanted.

I trip, catch myself,
stumble back from Time Remembered
to a chill in the air,
feel of first fall rain.
I peer down at the mysterious creek
on its way to the sea,
but smile to myself, and at returning wife and dog.
Then homeward,
a man on his birthday blessed,
walking among the bright presents of the world.

On Language

ON MY 75TH BIRTHDAY

I wake up wondering why
there is something rather than nothing,
but grateful, grateful
for this body which carries
so much of my something.
This "frame," often achy
and always a little slow,
has been my strict teacher.
Thank you, professor,
for pleasure, for pain,
for letting me know
"The lyf so short,
the craft so long to lerne."

ANOTHER TEACHER

Rain steady on the roof. Far shore lost.
Sea – quiet, gray, introspective – *like me*,
I think, entering from stage left.
This is what we've made language for,
to enter the world's drama as player,
not just reflex towards food,
away from the saber-tooth.

On the table beyond my book,
an off-white bowl holds three oranges
and an Asian pear. Eye takes them up.
Mind calls for a palate of words.
Suddenly the undertones of blue
on the skin of the pear and the green shadows
beneath the mandarins reveal themselves.
Praise Language for showing eyes
what they have seen.

WORDS AND THINGS

       Midsummer. Where the stream no longer moves,
a skin of algae floats, but where the current is still,
swift, thick ropes of riverweed turn – deep, green,
sinuous in the dark water, swaying with the water's
rush, catching the flickering, hypnotic pattern
of what passes. They are a mirror more knowing than one
that merely turns our outer selves back to our inner eye.

"Words are the daughters of earth," said Johnson,
then added "But things are the sons of heaven."
We are stepchildren of their marriage, sometimes
favoring the daughters, sometimes the sons.

On the Way to Canterbury

We wake up wondering –
in those grand morning tootings,
that pulling together of what
the eye sees with where
the mind goes, that shuffling
through the volumes
of the dreamed and lived life –
what's it all for?
and while wondering
we watch the words walk together
like pilgrims, each with a story,
each with a holy purpose.

Wouldn't it be good to join them
like the tavern keeper,
and listen to their tales
as they go their way,
not write like an impresario
arranging great moments.

CREATION

Never think of surface except as an extension of volume.

Auguste Rodin

The old book said God was the first
sculptor – shaping us out of clay
using himself as model – there was
no one else. But God had so much
volume, he had no surface. He was
just every where.

      He'd done a lot
of work on creation already, time, universes
and such, finishing things up now, teaching
himself along the way, yet all that he made
was part of him.

      Bending to breathe life
into these new ones, He thought to withhold
himself, to leave in each a place, simply
where he was not – an ending, a surface,
his own surface. I will call that
not-me-ness *Soul*, thought God, for the first time
needing a name.

      Until then, God
had no need of language. He did not say,
"Let there be light." That was a scribe trying
to understand creation, but He/She – already
you can see the trouble with words – held light

and dark within. The Eternal, being all,
did not need to say "this is like that"
to understand the nature of things. Ah,
but Eve's "Mmm" at the apple was more
than a cat's purr, and Adam's "Mmm, Mmm"
not only enjoyed the juice, but said,
"I'm twice as good at this sinning as you."

Those angels who drove us from the garden
made sort of a humming sound which we
translated as "Hosanna" – as we set off being fruitful,
multiplying, speechifying. When we began
to write poems, God learned how to read.
When we began to sing, God heard
discord and harmony and understood
how they worked together.

FALL CLEANING

Books read, unread, and never-to-be-read,
jottings, the remains of paid bills, old tax forms,
unopened software, letters years old still
to be answered, manuals, CD's, Judith's note
saying Cecily's ballet class has been canceled
20 years ago, a picture of my mother, in her 30's,
standing by Arthur Melrose dressed in a dinner jacket.
Outside the frame of the picture, a 1-1/2 X 2-1/2,
black and white, fading, live his brothers, and Helen
and Jennie, his sisters – and Jennie's Model T with
the rumble seat ancient even then and her picking me
up at the train station at Huntington, Long Island,
the clatter of her car louder than the great diesel.

Morning after. Everything spread about looking
for order, for boxes, for trash cans, for attention.
I lie in bed reading Jorie Graham, "The earth curves
more than I had thought /at first." Yesterday sinks
just beyond the horizon. I poke among the seaweed
for what is cast up, left, from the shipwreck of each day.

DOWN IN THE DUMPS

So, a man is down in the dumps – not
cast down – just where he ends up after
a long walk through morning and afternoon.

Day has gone, but evening has not yet come.
Here is where all the marvelous stuff – the spring-sprung
rumble seat, the milk wagon whose wooden horse

is missing a leg, dried cheese wrappers, rusting
tomato soup cans, gutted paper backs, scraps of journals –
are heaped together, no longer propped up by usefulness.

He is no longer useful. He feels kin to the toaster with the broken
cord lying on its side like a double-mouthed bottom creature tossed
from the sea. And all of the bottles losing their labels – no longer

wine shapes or mayonnaise shapes but collocations of curve, line,
and shadow. He too is losing his labels and sits on a bucket feeling
supple as a seal. He watches a vortex of seagulls whirl

and settle on the fuming heaps picking, picking with strong
yellow beaks. One has only one leg, but it squawks
and bobs as hungrily as the rest. The man picks up

the shade of a bottle and, is it a hacksaw handle? Chink, they
go together, and *chink-chink*, and *chinkety-chinkety-chaw-chaw*.
This is the melody of the blue hour. It is not melancholic.

Soon the moon will come, but She is not what he's waiting for.
He is waiting for nothing. He is banging a bottle with his lost
wooden horse leg, *chinkachink-achinkety-chaw-chaw-chaaah!*

FEEDING THE WOLF

Five A.M. and the dictator is up
strutting about the balcony giving orders
of order. He is pleased with himself.
His clocks strike an accurate hour –
but no service is civil. So, rebellious
artists roam about the countryside
painting the horses mauve, and a small boy
has begun to bring his porridge
to the edge of the forest to feed the wolf.

CHU TA

    could only live high or low.
Drunk, he'd paint illogical landscapes,
fish glowering out of square eyes,
sparrows teetering on a single leg.
Yet sometimes a fluffy, unnameable,
satisfied bird preened happily
in a corner. To write, he'd grab
a brush and bellow like a madman.
One day, he hung on his door
the sign for dumb and never
spoke again. This is what
was said when he died, "Alas,
Alas, one can get drunk as he
did, but not crazy as he was."

So It Is

A nobleman conceals a spent fox
beneath his robe till the hunters pass by –
later he meets a beautiful woman,
marries her, and she bears a son.

But after three years, her skin crawls
at the touch of silk. Even the smell
of her own child is sharp in her nose,
so she leaves to become fox again.

Yoshitoshi's print shows her departure,
her son holding on to her robe,
her profile, shadowed in the sliding
paper door, already fox.

Thinking of the Thinking of the Models of Matisse

What to make of all these naked ladies some
in blue, some lined out – legs crossed, one arm
behind the head to shift the weight of one breast up-
ward, while the other hangs out with gravity.

Their faces are abstracted, introspective –
"Well, this is what the old guy wants,"
they seem to say. "Well, I'll give it to him.
He's paying – If he wants shape, I'll give

him shape, the old cut-up, but nothing
else of me." The Master nods his head,
points his beard harrumphs "Don't move,"
and though the rump on which most of

their weight rests aches, they're still till the scissors
are done, or his blue brush, or his sure, inky line.

At the Uffizi, Things Are As They Are

Rembrandt, looking in a mirror thinks:
Life has drawn such a face on me
and I too can draw it out of the darkness.

In the tratoria, a Modigliani pulls the lever
on the espresso machine. Her hair is dark as coffee.
Her skin shines like an olive on a white plate.

The olive trees march towards the sea –
single file along a trail cut into the hillside
– like legionnaires on a bivouac.

The Romans called that "great wink' Mare Nostrum;
the empire fell. Regardless, the white horses
of Neptune plunge toward the shore.

On her seashell the Lady rides – her face
as new as Eve's when first pulled from Adam's side.
When Venus steps ashore, our time begins.

The Coronation of Mary is always happening
and if some saints and angels turn to look at us for awhile,
after the snapshot's taken, they turn again to adoring.

Here, Kronos is eating his children. Rembrandt,
looking in the mirror, sees the mark of his tooth.
He does not look away. He will see things as they are.

THE FACE OF REMBRANDT

Walking through the Uffizi,
Bemused by all those bright images,
cherubs at mischievous worship,
gods and goddesses at their naked play –
we come near the end to the face Rembrandt
painted of the face of Rembrandt.

Standing before a mirror, he saw
from the shadows, eyes looking out at him.
Where had those eyes gone
to look out of such a face?

Needing to know
he took up his brush....

ON CEZANNE

Some can hear a hundred pitches
in the scale that we say has twelve.

So Cezanne saw a thousand shades
of green and blue as if they were
narcissus and reflection,
one breathing air, the other water.

When the child paints the grass blue,
the sky green, he's correcting the teacher
whose eyes have grown dull from defining.

DIEBENKORN AT THE OAKLAND MUSEUM

Figure on a Porch

Woman on a porch
in the full gold of summer.
She has risen from her chair
to stare away from us
over the green fields,
over the dark blue bay.
The tilt of her head
suggests her eyes are lifted
beyond the low dark-
green headlands
to a light-blue sky.

The intense world is here,
almost in the shapes
eye is accustomed to,
but Euclid, the god
of the rectangle,
has reached out his brush.

"The world," he says,
"Is pattern and particular.
Let me show you both."

Ocean Park 107

Almost all grown
to geometry now
out of which
something shines.

At the Academy

Things are themselves, but also shapes –
the flat rectangles of these bedroom walls,
the contoured cylinder of the coffee thermos,
the humped cartography of the white comforter.
So eye flickers between the particular and
abstract. At the Academy, Plato points
to the heavens, Aristotle to the earth.

MAUREEN PLAYS BACH

Outside, above tulips and sea lavender,
hummingbirds – their wingbeats
swift and sweet as a trill.

In here, Bach wants Maureen's fingers
to move just so.
She cannot think them
where to go,

so, he waves his baton
from the swelling
at the top of the spine
where Will shows Desire
how to enter the World.

That's where we store the learned,
the practiced virtues –
riding a bicycle,
feel of a pinch of salt,
"Sarabande from Suite A."

Playing the Piece

Art Tatum: "There's no such thing as a wrong note,"
and Don Byas explaining,
"What makes a note wrong is when
you don't know where to go after that one.
You hit one. If it's not right,
you hit another. If that's not right,
you hit another, so you just keep hitting.
Now who's going to say you're wrong?
As long as you keep on going, you're all right,
but don't stop, because if you stop you're in trouble.
Don't ever stop unless you know you're at a station."

THIS IS A POLITICAL POEM

from Piano Shop on the Left Bank

Three people stand in a shop in Paris looking
at an old piano. It might have been played by
Beethoven. The veneer is sumptuous, though
blistered where separated from the shaping
pieces. Inside, no cast-iron frame, but thick,
wooden struts. The woman attempts a scale, but
many of the notes are missing. "It's like trying
to capture moonlight in a net." The man marvels
at the piano's age and that it had been made
entirely by hand. The shop owner tells them,
"The trees for the wood were most likely planted
in the late sixteenth century. The woodworking
guilds of Germany planted trees so their children's
children's children would have the right kind of wood
harvested, sometimes, 250 years later. Then it was
cured from 10 to 40 years. Even in the nineteenth century,
such wood was rare, but now it is a substance
that has gone out of the world we live in."

Go Way From My Window

I'm sitting in a bar – drinking a martini larger than I'd
make at home – because I do not want to drink alone. I am, of course,
drinking alone.

I like the noises, the "warm, drunken wash of voices," the beat of
the bad music just beneath disturbing loud – I'm aware that the gin is good
and I'm aware that I'm thinking of Gladys Swarthout when she came to
Danville, Kentucky in the fall of 1950 to perform at the basketball court
which four times a year doubled as a ballroom and once in a blue moon as
a concert hall. I'm sitting in the bleachers listening, something to do in a
town and time when any something was better than the usual nothing.

I float above the clinking beer glasses remembering how
beautiful and exotic she was – broad-chested, dark-haired, big-voiced,
and I remember wondering what we were both doing there. I was sitting
next to my roommate, also from New York, who in the spring would
serenade the girl's dorm singing "Some Enchanted Evening" in his fine
baritone, and when his former girl would not come down and join him
(these were the days of girl's dorm lockdowns and house mothers and the
like, and it was maybe two in the morning, his voice muzzy with drink)
brought out a pistol full of threats. He waved it around and shortly after
waved goodbye to the school.

One could say "girl's dorm" then; Breckinridge Hall was the boy's
dorm in turn. The returning GI-billed soldiers lived in Vet's Village, ran
a never-stopping card game, and supported a steady trickle of moonshine
from the hills. I was 16 and a long way from home which mostly felt good.

I can't remember the first part of her program – maybe some 19th
century German art songs about babbling brooks and the beloved which

I likely wasn't ready for. At the end she sang, "Sometimes I Feel Like a Motherless Child" which explored a place in me I didn't know existed, and then, "Go Way From My Window" :

> Go way from my window
> Go way from my door
> Just leave me with my broken heart
> And bother me no more,
> And bother me no more.
>
> I'll give you back your diamonds,
> I'll give you back your rings
> But I'll ne'er forget the love we knew
> As long as song birds sing,
> As long as song birds sing.

her big voice carrying passion so darkly that no sweet-voiced folk-song singer could seduce me a decade later.

My drink is gone, though the ice cubes I suck on are reminiscing about the good times with the good gin. I could have another, but it would not be as good. I know that, but I'm still tempted.

FOR CHARLENE

Those ancients who heard
beyond the changing moon
the sweet sounds
of the planets' singing,
and the poet who wrote,
"From harmony, from heavenly harmony
This universal frame began,"
knew something of music,
how it surrounds us, impels us,
how out of its cadences, something new
in us is born. So, we come together
to sing, to do our best,
but are not wise enough
to know what best can be.

So, bring on the conductor with her magic wand.
Let her be tall and graceful, yet stern as fate.
Let her ear be tuned to the planets
and her mind to what the words are saying.
Let her make us turn aside
from the seduction of the good enough.
Let her make us lose ourselves in the music.

Stand straight. Out she strides on stage.
The audience applauds. She turns to us,
smiles, raises an eyebrow, a baton. We begin.

POEM FOR MY FATHER'S BIRTHDAY

When I was so small
You could hurl me to heaven
And catch me when the angels missed,
You stood tall as a ship
That could sail to China
And blow home before supper.
When you were so big
You could hold back the sunset
Or spin the moon on the back of your hand,
I was so small
I could run in your shadow
And never reach the end of it.

One night when Long John Silver
Swore and threw his crutch
Of lightning across the sky
And the thunder of his guns assaulted us
Until our windowpanes shook with fright
And the maddened horse of a wind
Almost ran us down as it tried to escape,
You put your man's hand
On the back of my neck
And found words to ease me
So that when the rain bullets came,
I could enjoy my trembling.

1990/1946

Soon I will be older than my father
when he died. How often I've thought – I'm forty.
What was he doing when he was forty?
or forty five? fifty? when he was this age
or that he was doing . . . and I would fill in
the blank part memory, part imagination.

Sometimes I see me there too and try
to hold his mind in mine while thinking
back into the mind I wore then – like now,
mother away, I come as my father, day-shift
foreman at Mack Motors and worried about me,
and I come as me just worried, starting high school,
and we meet at the White Tower, eat thin hamburgers,
sliced pickles, comforting fried onions.

DRIVING TO WORK

My father's behind the wheel.
His silhouette glowing in the gray morning light –
big man, straight gray hair,
slope of second chin beneath his first,
powerful hands, shoulders,
belly pushing towards the steering wheel.
6:45 A.M. Two-lane road
from town to town
between square, Ohio farms.

Whispers of mist float
between the stones
of the River Junction graveyard.
Sometimes I drink a beer alone
in that town's tavern.

We don't need to talk,
the air that sweet between us.

Forty years gone.
I've made my living all that time by talking.
Now I sit in Maine looking out of a window over a lake,
sun still below the horizon,
but stretching his limbs,
water deep in shivery, morning thought.

Neither one of us liked our jobs –
my father fallen, and I
had not found a way to rise,
but we drove together
early in the morning
with such a sweetness between us.

LEARNING FROM MY FATHER

in the foundry, watching great ladles of metal swing out of the dark furnace and trolley across the plant high above our heads, the deep orangey red of iron, the thin shiny bright yellow of brass, my father's crew tipping the pots of fire into the molds more carefully than ever my mother poured coffee. this is the only life for a man, I think, the heating of metal and the pouring of it – or maybe

that life is like when my father would drive a fire engine home, flashing up the driveway, siren whooping, shiny red it would be, with a trim of real gold, gold leaf three hundreths of an inch thick inlaid over the thick paint, the hand-rubbed coats of radiant paint, and my father driving it, one hand on the wheel, one hand flicking the thong to the great silver bell,

or maybe I learned that from my father's hand - big with use, thumbnail irredeemably cracked, arm, shoulder, back that once knew how to make things move.

we played this game. he would place his thumb and four fingers against the large tendons of my neck and squeeze. when I said "ow," game over. "ows" came quickly, yet older and stubborner and into myself, the pain lengthened. at maybe 13, I did not say "ow" though there was no stint of squeezing.

no cruelty here. affection. the touch of his hand good, yet maybe the lesson not good.

when anger came, his throat narrowed until sound could not get out nor air get in.

THIS WONDER

Christmas morning. I wake early
to a strange noise from below,
and, in my footed pajamas, holding
on to the railing, I creep down the
shadowy stairs leading from the
chauffeur's flat to the workroom
below. Of all things, there's my
father bending over an electric train
whizzing round and round an oval
track nailed to a piece of plywood.
He doesn't see me, but I watch him
caught as he is in the mystery of train
lights, ruby and white, circling in
the half-darkness. For awhile I don't
make a sound, but watch him,
wondering about his strange smile.

All these years later, I tiptoe down
the stairs again, now understanding
the poverty of his childhood
and the jobless years of the Depression,
and I watch him and imagine him thinking –
I am able
> *to give to my children,*
> *for Christmas,*
>> *this wonder.*

TALKING WITH MOTHER YOUNG, OLD

She is the whole parade, the bands, the strutting
twirlers, the orange blossom queens waving
from their silver floats. We are the audience
lining the streets, expected to applaud each new
and passing act – but, we cannot clap enough,
so the streets turn empty, the city – cardboard
for the Tsar. Dusk. A little girl wanders, crying, lost.

Mother, drifting in and out of sleep, starts, wakes,
says, "We're sitting in the barn with all the cows."
She must have fled there sometimes as a girl
from her troubled house. Is that the heaven
she'd run to now, back to the barn by the lake
and the heavy stir of those radiant creatures,
the sweet incense of milk, straw, dung?

ORPHANS OF THE STORM

We scrambled up the bank of the old feeder canal,
that rose behind our new house leaving food warm
in the kitchen and the dining room table set for guests.
We stood looking below as the Greater Miami River
slid up the street, reached our house, pushed in
the basement windows and made itself at home.
As we slogged along the overgrown trail
mother began to smile and wave at the neighbors
standing below in their front yards watching
the water seek out house after house. At last
she called out, "We're Orphans of the Storm,
Orphans of the Storm," now not an extra, but the star.

WHILE WALKING THE DOG

Thinking about Mother while walking the dog,
thinking that Helmer came at last to whisper
"I'll be loving you always" as he did once
after months of silence to heal their courting,

thinking she reached out her hand to his
and left the body which had missed him for
forty years, left the right leg with its
inserted pin still almost shiny, left

her left leg with its partial hip replacement,
left her blind eye, her wheelchair and got up
to dance the hambo to a friendly
accordion among the other Swedes

who, young again, whirl round and round
at the heavenly Gota Lejon Temperance Lodge.

BILL'S HAT

FOR BROTHER BILL [1936–2004]

I'm walking under
Bill's hat
in the Highlands.

Bill wore many hats
in his life. Which
fit best? A mystery.

I think of him
handsome, skinny –
long hair swept back

from a high brow,
almost a ducktail –
working after school

at Country Club Motors.
How he loved the gleam
of fender, hum of engine,

the talk in the salesmen's shack.
I'm not saying this
could have been a life,

I'm saying: this
was a hat he wore,
and, for awhile, it fit.

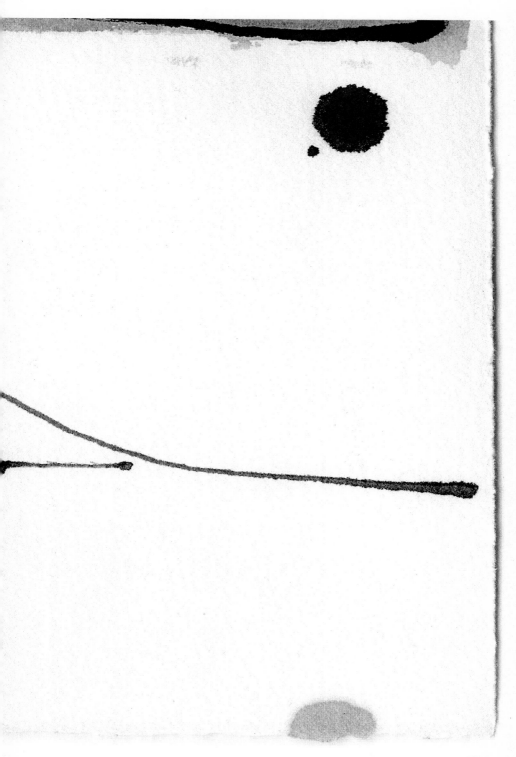

6.20.03

For Abby Niebauer

I remember your dark brown eyes
and your pale freckled skin
and your frizzly redbrown hair
and the black cotton summer dress
      with the small white polka dots
      you wore when we had our long talk,
and I remember how your hands
         and feet – larger than their body – gave you a
graceful earnest awkwardness that would not
let me speak too easily, and I remember the fragility
of that body beneath my hands
      the one time we tried to dance.

and yes, I remember a small flat
      place on the end of your lovely nose.

THAT'S THE BALL GAME

A single – but Russ, knees high, pumping hard, leaned round first with never a stop thought as the right fielder overran then fumbled the ball, *and when the whole body sings with moving why drop anchor at second,* so by the time the short stop caught, wheeled, and heaved it wide, Russ was hell-bent for home as any voyager, ready to barrel into the catcher who simply stepped aside when no throw came.

Wrapped in a warm summer cocoon of stadium light, the three of us cheered from the bleachers, my friends halfway between me and Russ in years, beginning to mourn their distance from the carelessness of the young body, from the confidence that this day's bruise will be gone by tomorrow, from the understanding that life would offer no hurt more than a bruise, from the conclusion: *Why not run heedless – breath comes easy, flesh is immortal, the last obstacle will step aside, there'll be friends to cheer.*

Morning in Montana, June, 1993

for Bill Stafford [1914–1993]

Someone's opened the cabin door
and stands a shadow between
the stove air and the mountain
cold. He runs his hands along

the doorposts then up across
the lintel seeming to measure,
seeming to feel for its shape
and size. It is Bill Stafford.

He vanishes, then reappears,
his hands again searching
to know this door. He senses
my open eyes, then really

disappears. Later I ask,
was it you? what were you doing?
He smiles at me and will not
admit and will not explain.

PENELOPE

This time, it is Penelope who goes off
while Odysseus stays home to mind the kingdom,
not to a war, but to the wedding of a special
girlhood friend married off to a barbarian
to seal a treaty. Then things kept coming up,
for twenty years – not monsters so much, though
sometimes monstrous things. This is a life, after all.

The god she angered was Zeus who preferred
that women stay at home, but he largely ignored her
having his own affairs to tend to. So, mostly
she lost her handmaidens through natural causes,
cholera, accident, love. She lost none to Scylla or
Charybdis, giving herself time to sail around. The sirens?
They ignored her. No need to waste music on a sister.
Oh, yes, there was a man on whose island she spent
some time. Though it was clear he was no immortal,
sometimes he made her feel as if she might be.

Towards the end, tired of the gypsy life, she
traded her last jewel for passage home. The curious
Phoenicians thought this dusty, graying woman claiming
to be queen a little daft as they rowed her ashore, but queen
she was, for an old woman curtsied and an old dog, for once
not barking, stretched out its gray head. At the palace, she
found her husband besieged by women wanting to be queen.

Odysseus had been faithful in his own way,
favoring one woman, then another, weaving relationships
at night which he undid in the morning. He had always
expected his wife to come back. At her entrance, the suitors
sniffed at this unlikely female, but when the king rose
and bowed, they turned, gathered perfumes, robes,
ornaments, and scattered like bats at dawn to isles
where royalty might be a little less canny. That night,
the wife and husband lay down in their ancient bed
each wondering how much they should say to each other.

To the Storyteller, On Having Found One of Her Secrets

Dear Gioia,

Reading the Odyssey, I looked up from my page
and saw, suddenly, with my inner eye, you, dressed
in black, staring out of a window somewhere, Maine, maybe,
offering the audience your strong profile. You were as deep
in yourself as one can go and keep a clear trail back.

I had been reading those verses where the hero
digs a trench, surrounds it with milk, honey, wine, water, barley,
then cuts the throats of a ram and black ewe. Dark blood
falls into the earth wound. Then out of Erebus eager souls
erupt, longing to drink, longing to wear again the sweet cloak
of flesh. There's only one story Odysseus must hear and one
who knows the story, so the hero waits, sword drawn, thrusting
away friend, mother. At last, the shade of Tiresias, "And once
he had drunk the dark blood, the words came ringing
from the prophet in his power."

Now it was as if I found the path you had taken
and followed you inward, coming at last to a shore
by the wine-dark sea where a thousand tales erupted
from the earth. You stood there holding the fierce sword
of your attention, listening, as the stories scuffled
with each other crying for attention, for the one that must
be told at this time, in this place, and I saw one
of your great secrets, that presence to the moment
of the telling, the knowledge that when the right
story comes, one's words come ringing forth
like those from a "prophet in his power."

ON ROBERTA'S BOOK

Pictures bound in the center, first
of a beautiful child,
ringlets, dark big eyes,
small assured curves at the corners
of her mouth. She is the princess
of a land which loves her.
In the fourth picture, grown
to a lovely woman, she looks
as if life were giving her all,
all she wanted, all she deserved,
the only cost her curls.
Yet by the fifth she has begun
to draw a greatcoat of flesh about
her shoulders as if to fend off
an unimaginable cold.
Now that she is dead,
her poems crowd around grieving.
Some weep outright.

Once my older daughter
then four and visiting Daddy at the office
looked up at her and said,
    "You are a fat lady,"
and in the unpossessed silence, again,
    "You are a fat lady."
From atop the great mountain of herself
Roberta peered down and said,
    "Yes, my dear, I am a fat lady."

POEM FOR FREDERICK

Driving back from a night at the shore
between hills green with new rye grass. Home,
I see in my neighbor's yard the year's first
iris bud. The purple of that almost-here
flower, makes me remember that Frederick
wanted a winter poem by tonight for *The Crow.*

Well, here it is, a day late, finished up
in a coffee shop, Super Bowl Sunday,
temperature in the fifties, air moist,
low gray clouds moving in a slow scud.
There's skiing three hours drive away
I won't go, yet I have "a mind of winter."

Well again. It isn't finished. I type
a week later. Now jonquils and daffodils,
and when I walk my dog, I see heron – like
white clouds – nesting in a still-barren tree.
Yet my winter mind dozes in its burrow
refusing to come out of long sleep.

Three or four years later, still not finished,
and you now sleep the longest sleep. Frederick,
this year I missed the gravity of your smile in the dining hall
where we once leaned on coffee and waited for sunrise.
So fierce you were against injustice, at such a cost.
You would not dance, but there was such a longing in you.

A KIND OF BIOGRAPHY

All night the language dog
gnaws at the meaning bone.

Soon the sea begins
to question its shuffling

from East to West, and the stars
their vast, ordinary circuits.

So my friend has fled
into his father's fields.

He leans against a fence
and wonders what the ant means

and the moonlit grasses as they bend
and spread and flow beneath

a wind whose beginning seems obscure
and whose end, uncertain.

He notices that something of himself
has set off with the wind

and that he is now two.
He wonders at this doubleness.

Back home, he sits in the kitchen,
an ordinary boy watching

his mother cook breakfast,
but something of him is in

another place, and some other thing
is with him even here.

ROBERT, GRAVEL-VOICED

Robert, gravel-voiced, comes in the night.
Fierce or friendly? Who can tell? He gives
me a copy of his new book. It is several
of his small books, signed but unsold at his
readings, bound together. "Work," he growls
at me, "Work." I nod and agree, but he is
dissatisfied. "Read page 330," he grumbles.
"But there is no page 330." "Work!"

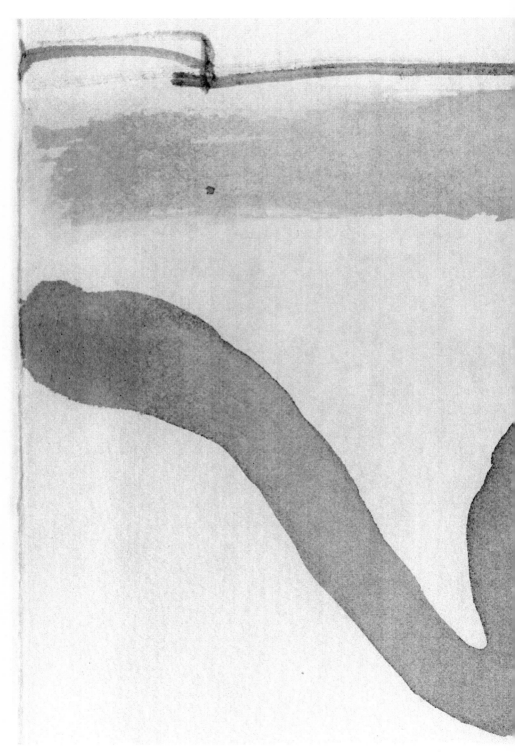

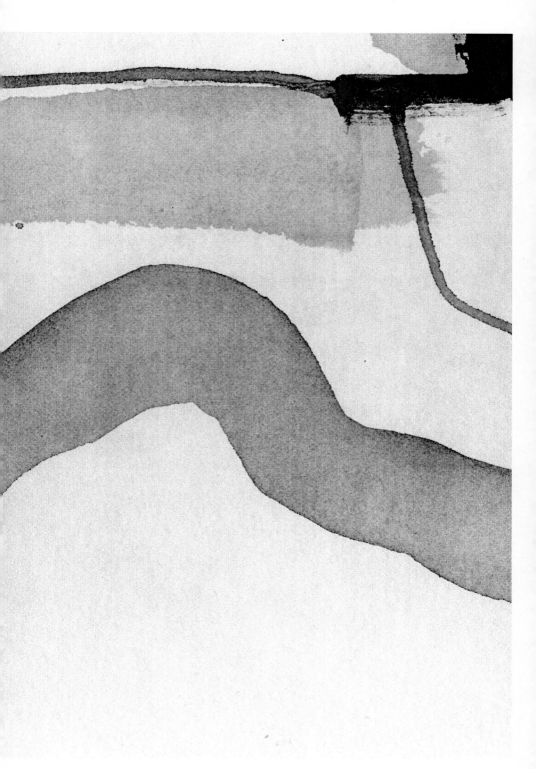

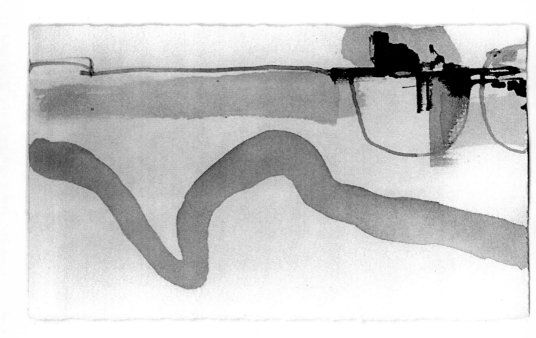

COFFEE SHOP IN THE LATE AFTERNOON

The beautiful woman gone
leaving the shop to young men making
their way in the January world
with cell phones and computers –

and me.

Outside, a sunny day.
too warm for the season.

A phone rings – a barista calls out
"Tall vanilla soy latte."
Strange talk to one who grew up
with a nickel cup of joe.

There are fewer and fewer
native speakers of one's born language.

You learn to live with translations.

LONELINESS

Bus across the fells of Mull – road, a single lane between hills barren, brown – hardly a sheep to note our coming. Bus mostly filled with the collared clergy, heavy-voiced, though on retreat – and some chattering women of the church. I feel superior, particularly to one collar who again and again stands in the lurching aisle to bring information about car rentals and ferry prices to those not terribly wanting to hear. "I've got the brochure in my bag," he says again and again to faces dressed in politeness. Then I see the tweed coat around his black dickie is old, and its bottom seam unstrung and my heart eases towards him.

In the middle of nothing the bus stops, and a woman I had not noticed rises carrying a sleeping red-haired boy over her shoulder. She gets off. My eyes follow her down a road I had not seen, to a farm I had not seen – a trailer and some fencing at the end of a rocky path. She does not look back as our gears grind and we lunge forward. Years later I think of her loneliness, and the loneliness of the small red-haired boy when he awoke, and of the loneliness of the clergyman, and of loneliness.

How Things Come Apart

It's all over between you and a woman. Wife, maybe. Long time live-in lover. Whatever. It's all over. And you go over to your old house, which she has, or your old apartment to pick up a few things – extra pots for your new kitchen, or an unneeded rug, maybe a sweater you left in the closet or the good sock found at last, and all of a sudden it happens. Desire sweeps over you and there you are making the best love you've ever made in your life, the two of you who couldn't even speak to each other the week before without calling down curses from the gods are rolling about the bed or humping on the floor – or table top even, and it's terrific, better than its ever been, better than the first time you hopped into the sack, or second or third, rather, when it's still new but you've gotten to know each other's bodies a little and have a sense of how things go best. But now, when it's over, there's this one time and it's never been better.

Night now and you're back in your new place, alone, wondering, listening to music, the Modern Jazz Quartet, caught in the sleepy accurate bass of Percy Heath, and it comes to you that it had to do with time, this magic time between past and future, tide just turned, after midnight but tomorrow not yet today. The past has run its course, the threads of its responsibilities woven together, knotted. The future has not yet beginning its knitting, – free time, – and the liberated beast exults, living again without consequence as if before the fall, or between falls – or,

if falling, it is Sisyphus and Sisypha, humming a little tune, their own tune, "The Lay of the Last Lay," walking down the mountain hand in hand, doing a dance, a happy hitch step, amused at their furious bodies up above there some place having joyfully at each other,

not yet thinking of the bottom of the hill where each one's next stone waits.

SOMETIMES A MAN DISAPPEARS

Sometimes a man disappears from a village
or a city-woman leaves her flat and is seen
no more. A boy goes off on an errand,
a girl leaves for school and that's it. They're gone.

Not important people, not long remembered,
save, maybe one of the old folk, thinking back
over a long life, will catch a shadow
of memory and wonder – but not for long.

Last night I came back from a dream, some
fully-lived life, the movement through time
the same as this movement. I think wife,
children, and an unexceptional job.

But I woke in this place. Back there, an old one
may ask, *What became of that tall, thin, quiet man.*

WHAT I LEARNED FROM MY YEARS AT SEA

The Northwest Passage

Emily Dickinson called one of the hallways in her house "The Northwest Passage." Was it the one that led to or from her room? – the same space, but direction matters – a shortcut to somewhere – but an icy one. Maybe it was the way to the parlor where the critic sat in his black vested suit.

I see her brave trim ship caught in the ice. I see her harnessing the dogs. I follow her across the white of days and the light-empty nights. At last she arrives – stretches out her cold hand, says, "How kind of you to call, Mr. Higginson."

Iceberg

Danish parsons preached that a trip to the North Pole would be good for the soul, but being from a practical race understood that such a journey was unlikely – cold sea, icebergs, vast sheets of snow – maybe impossible. Yet, no doubt the soul would grow on such a trip.

Finally, the most pragmatic of priests declared that any trip, even the short sail from Copenhagen to Malmo was, "properly considered," a journey to the North Pole.

The moral is that icebergs are where you find them, that many a Titanic has foundered in the living room, but, if you sail past, round the Pole and return, your soul likely will have grown.

What I Learned From My Years at Sea

What is real is the roll of the deck, the seawind spreading its wings across the great blue, the orders from above that you don't think about but do, and the understanding that the horizon is an imaginary line between above and below.

Brooding

Five P.M., high above Mutahar's Beach, the sea curving off and away in a "great wink of eternity," wondering if anyone read Hart Crane anymore. Talking with Sandra and Alan about how Hamlet comes into the play – the King talks, ambassadors talk, Laertes talks, Polonius talks, the Queen talks, the King talks some more, so in time the silent black Prince owns the loudest voice on the stage.

Sandra says, "You've got to talk about time," and I think about how plot is a special case of time – a way of looking at, say, a week as if it made sense. Next morning, I listen to Mingus improvising on the back of a record jacket – "Time is when a faucet dribbles from a leaky washer, [and] the owner of such has given up on the idea that the maintenance man is ever to change the rhythm beat of his leaky faucet ... before time runs out of time."

Sandra shows a video of 150 women sixty years and up dressed in white – hats, heels, – all white – making their solemnified way to the sea, down steep steps to the sea, hobbling and limping and striding across white sand towards the sea, to sit at white tables by the sea, to talk of time by the sea.

All the while I am remembering a day 3000 hours long.

And Bachelard calls out, "Every real poem ... contains the element of time stopped, time which does not obey the meter."

Einstein On Light, Love, Life

Light leaps
out of its star
going everywhere
in straight lines,
bending only
with its love
for matter.

The planets,
from the beginning,
anxious, longing,
in a spin,
turn one side,
then the other,
day after day,
wanting
to be touched
all over
by that sweetness.

We ride the rush
of that desire,
hanging on
for dear life,
light and dark,
light and dark,
light and dark.

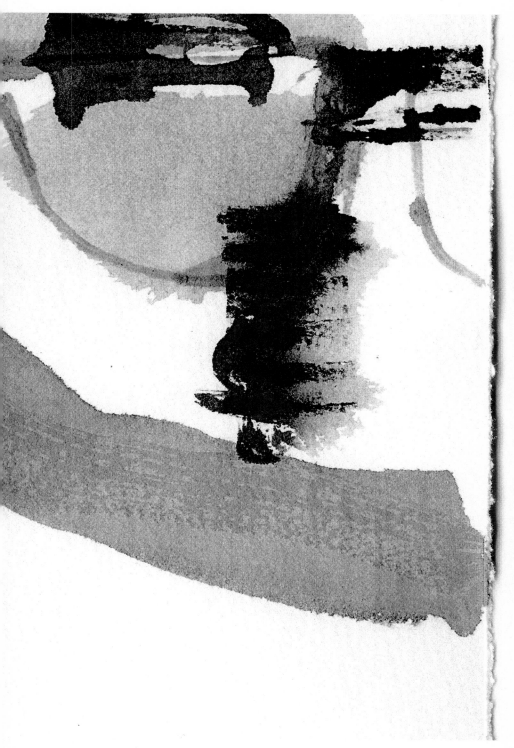

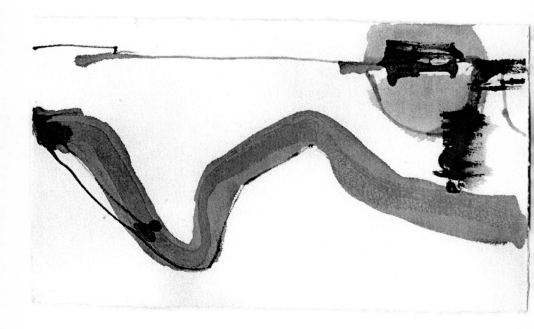

DITHYRAMB

A girl crosses the street
        behind two sullen boys,
her arms raised high
above her shoulders,
her fingers snapping to some tune
to which the twitch
of her skinny butt keeps time.

The ancient procession,
        the one before the actor
steps out and begins his talk,
        before tragedy and comedy
become two destinies,
        and there is just the walk
to the center of things
        to the music of the flute.

HOW THINGS HAPPEN

Rain comes when it will. It doesn't care for us.
It's hitchhiking its way to the sea on a cloud.
The sun is interested in its own fires. If light
comes, so be it. Bees feel an itch on their legs
only nectar can sooth. So many gifts from indifferent
givers. We walk through the world and smile,
remembering an old love, and Ramona, passing by,
thinks That man thinks I'm pretty, and walks in a way
that makes her more beautiful – and Henry,
walking down the street notices, makes a pass,
and they end up having a good marriage.

A Kiss

(from an anonymous Greek lyric)

I kissed a red lip
      and my own lip turned red.
I kissed a red lip
      and my own lip turned red.

      Wiped my lip on my sleeve,
           and my sleeve turned red.
      Wiped my lip on my sleeve,
           and my sleeve turned red.

Washed my shirt in the river
      and the river turned red
      and the edge of the shore
and red out even to the middle of the sea.

      An eagle flew down, touched water,
           and his wings turned red.
      He flew up and up
           and Lo! half the sun – red,

           and the whole of the moon.

Philosophy of Life, 201

In that class we were taught the attributes of God,
omniscience, omnipotence, omnipresence.
Out to the driveway for the paper this morning –
there a hawk in a nimbus of dove feathers.
At my footfall, he speared the carcass and carried it off.

Almost Advent – I've been brooding over that story,
the conception and birth, yes, but thinking of what's
to come, thinking God would have had to play fair
and not choose the life his son would lead. He would have had
to watch from the sidelines, caught in Time like
the rest of us. Oh, perhaps he loaded the dice a little,
good parents, a decent synagogue, but, to make sense,
the way of Jesus must have been of his own choosing.

Now I'm brooding on hawk and dove, guessing
God did not bring them together, though each
woke with a morning hunger. Hard to blame
the creator for that if one likes the idea of creation.
The hawk could have swung towards a mountain
mouse. The dove could have chosen another driveway.
"His eye is on the sparrow" speaks of attention,
not control. So, this morning I'm letting God
off the hook, giving up on omniscience and omnipotence,
though I seem to cling to omnipresence.

How To

The leaves outside my window shake with a deeper
movement than the continuing ripple of the light, morning,
midsummer breeze. "Squirrels," I think, and think
of how I know they're there although I cannot see them,
not a large movement, but enough if you paid
attention. This is how the ancients found the holy places,
then followed the ley lines that led from one to another.
Earth makes a gesture. Some subtle thing moves.
"Ah," you say, then "Ah" again, if you are paying
attention and mark where you are. Maybe you leave
a stone you've carried because it felt good in your hand.
Another person does the same. Soon there's a cairn,
then a cathedral where boys like me pay no
attention, but sing the mass beautifully anyway.

AT THE MILLPOND

A white bird flies low over its own white shadow.
When the bird rises, the shadow goes deep –
then disappears. When we rise, does not something
in us sink? The higher, the deeper.
When the shadow disappears, where are we
floating, then, so high above the earth?

Here Is No Ordinary Rejoicing

[For Bass, Tenor, and Two Choruses of Thousands]

Bass (Speaking): **Here is no ordinary rejoicing**

Tenor (chanting on any comfortable pitch):
    Let Ross, house of Ross rejoice with the great
    Flabber Dabber flat clapping fish with hands.

                            (Christopher Smart, *Jubilate Agno*)

The Choruses (speaking antiphonally)

Put down sackbut, psaltery, and cymbal.
Still the brazen mouth.
   Still,
     the trill,
the trill of the reed's tongue.
There is no measure we middling men may move to.
   No song,
     No dance,
No joy that can join
Can join, can join
       The rejoicing of Ross,
          Ross, Ross.

Be still you ordinary beasts!
   No belly roar of earthtop lumberer,
     No grind from a digger of darknesses,
       No honk from a waggler
         of wings in the high air
     Can counterpoint this chorus.

Only the Flabber Dabber mute fish
The Flabber Dabber gladder madder mute fish
 Can flap with his flukes
  Can clap with his flukes
   Can flip
    and flop
     and fling
      with his flukes

The Magnificat fish
Whose soul resounds in ways we cannot fish,
For he's the elate fish.
 Alloy
 Your joy
 Oh Ross
 With this great fish,
The one jubilate fish.

I WAKE ACHING

I wake aching from yesterday's mild exercise.
This body is not immortal, though,
sometimes I'm hard to convince.

If I came back, what would I be? –
something small, quick, and sly next time,
a night creature, fox maybe
or water rat, nose in the air, feet in water.

It is good to live in two worlds at once.

What lives between fire and earth?

or will we have no bodies then? just location?
like a point in geometry? I would miss this aging,
aching frame, the heaviness that anchors spirit
here in spring, like the pull of earth
that keeps the moon from swinging away.

Day's End

Oh yes, day was fine —
but now to bed. How good
to unbutton our approximate selves
and drop them on a chair,

The sheets make room for us then,
and the blankets lie ready to give back our warmth.
We read for awhile, then turn off the light
as night gathers us into her arms.

ACKNOWLEDGEMENTS

Versions of the following poems appeared in these journals:

DMQ Quarterly

Chu Ta, Fall Cleaning

New Universe News

This is a Political Poem

Northstar

Morning in Montana

Mildred

My Dog William and the Fence

Storyscape

On the Nature of Exposition

Driving a herd of Moose to Durango

To the Storyteller, Robert, Gravel-Voiced

National Poetry Review

A Kind of Biography

The Blue Sofa Review

Penelope, For Abby Niebauer, Talking with My Mother,
How Things Come Apart

Lighter Than Air

How Things Happen, At the Millpond

Cæsura
>Down in the Dumps, Feeding the Wolf

San Jose Studies
>On Roberta's Book

Red Wheelbarrow
>First Kiss, Loneliness, Poem for My Birthday

River Poet's Journal
>Go Way From My Window

It Has Come To This
>Poem for Frederick

Stymie
>Sandlots, Russ

Writer's Advice
>A Thing of Beauty

Knocking At The Door
>Creation

Beloit Poetry Journal
>Poem for My Father's Birthday

A Music Lover's Poetry Anthology
>For Charlene

Famous Writer's Anthology
>Ceremony

About the Author

Nils Peterson is Professor Emeritus at San José State University where he taught in the English and Humanities Departments. He has published poetry, science fiction, and articles on subjects as varying as golf and Shakespeare. He was nominated for a 2005 Pushcart Prize. A chapbook entitled *Here Is No Ordinary Rejoicing* was published by No Deadlines Press, *The Comedy of Desire* with an introduction by Robert Bly was published by the Blue Sofa Press, *Driving a Herd of Moose to Durango* appeared in 2005, *For This Day* in 2008, *Revenge of the Socks* in 2010, and *A Walk to the Center of Things* in 2011.

In 2009, he was chosen to be the first Poet Laureate of Santa Clara County.

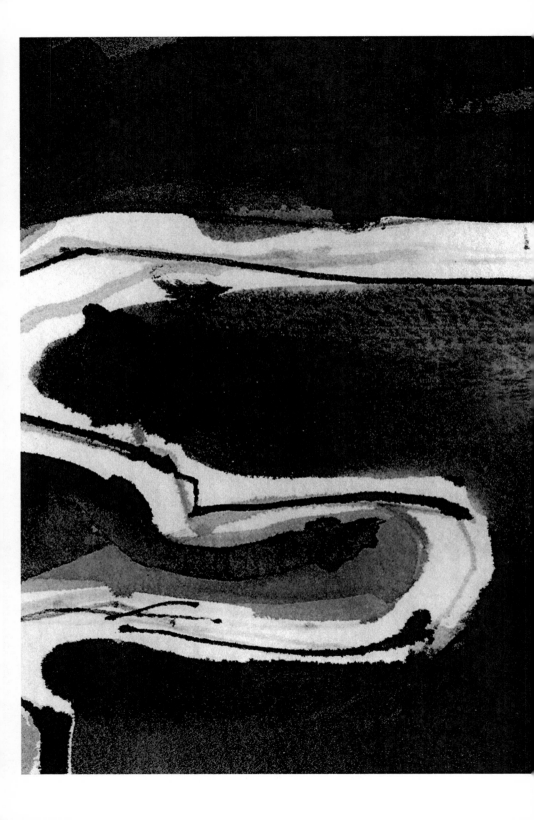